T.D. Jakes Speaks to Men:

Powerful, life-changing quotes to make you the man God intended you to be.

Bishop T. D. Jakes

T.D. Jakes Speaks to Men!
Powerful, life-changing quotes
to make you the man God
intended you to be.

ISBN 1-88008-986-6

Copyright © 1996 by T.D. Jakes
P.O. Box 7056
Charleston, West Virginia 25356

Published by ALBURY PUBLISHING
P.O. Box 470476
Tulsa, Oklahoma 74147-0406

Introduction

Few church leaders are ministering God's message of restoration and masculine identity to the needs of men today like T.D. Jakes. Bishop Jakes' biblical message on the true nature of manhood is a clarion call to the church.

We have tried to capture some of T.D. Jakes' most inspiring manhood messages in this convenient quote book. Whether it is read at home or during a break at work, it is our hope that these bite size nuggets of wit and wisdom will encourage men everywhere to celebrate their manhood

— WITH T.D. JAKES!

You must eat from the garden of your own thoughts. So don't grow anything you don't want to eat.

f there is anything worse than the rage, the frustration, and the other negative things that come out of us, it is the things that do not come out! Festering wounds are dangerous wounds.

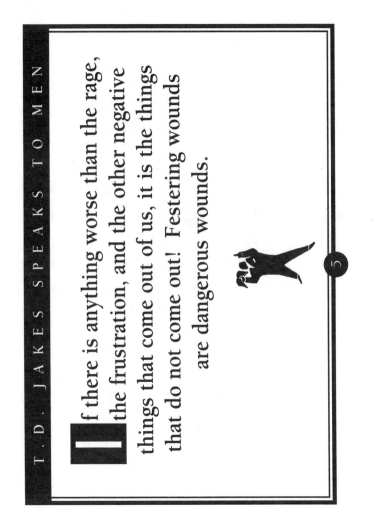

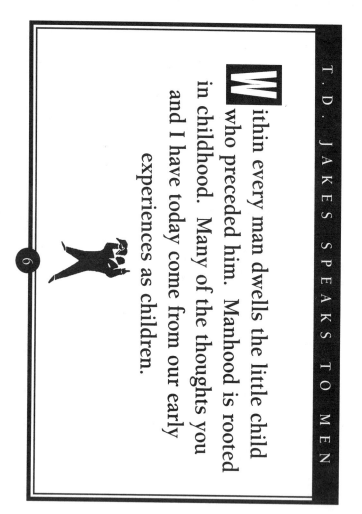

Within every man dwells the little child who preceded him. Manhood is rooted in childhood. Many of the thoughts you and I have today come from our early experiences as children.

6

We court disaster when we carry childish perceptions into adult relationships.

You will never understand the man I am on the outside until you have touched the child within me.

8

There is no room in the kingdom of God for macho men trying to impress one another with their collection of "toys" or "possessions." It doesn't matter whether these toys are cars, biceps, girlfriends, church members, or certificates of deposit. There is no room for this power struggle.

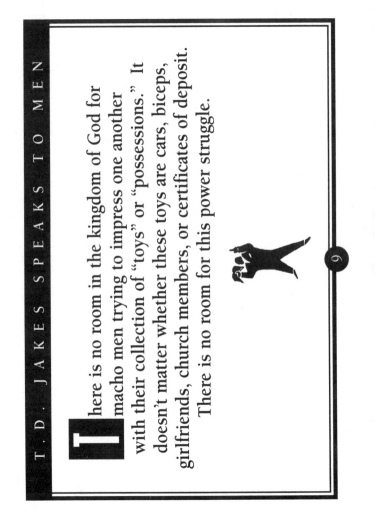

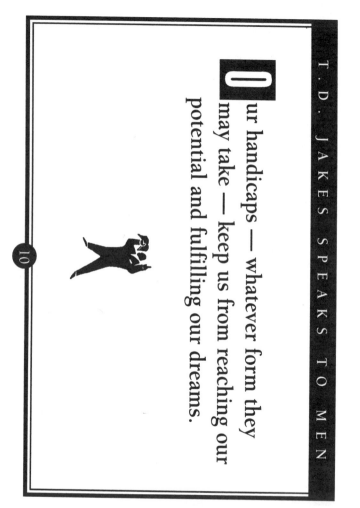

Our handicaps — whatever form they may take — keep us from reaching our potential and fulfilling our dreams.

Even our failures as Christian men are successes! They represent the miracle that you and I survived!

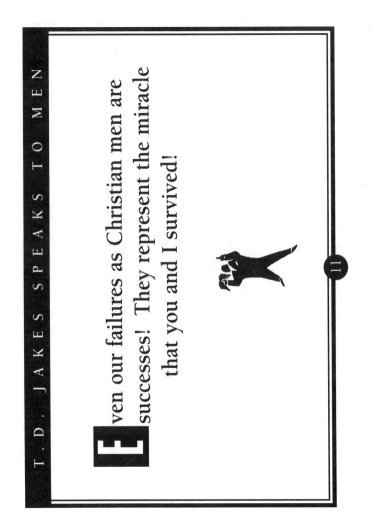

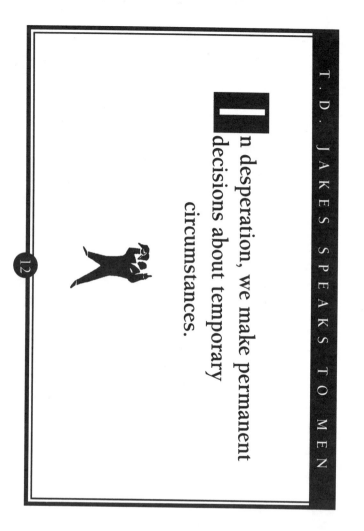

In desperation, we make permanent decisions about temporary circumstances.

We can no longer allow our past to destroy what God has for us in the present.

Only Jesus can walk us through the barrier of time to invade our past. There, He can make us comfortable with our uncomfortable parts and at peace with our frailties and brokenness.

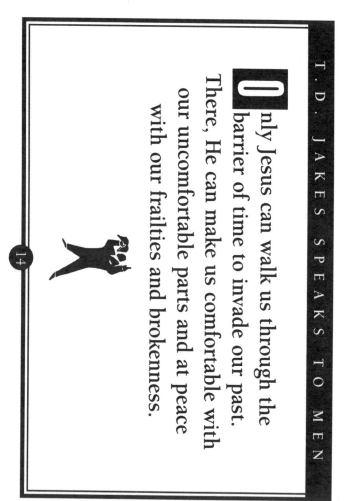

You can never become what you want to be until you can drop who you used to be.

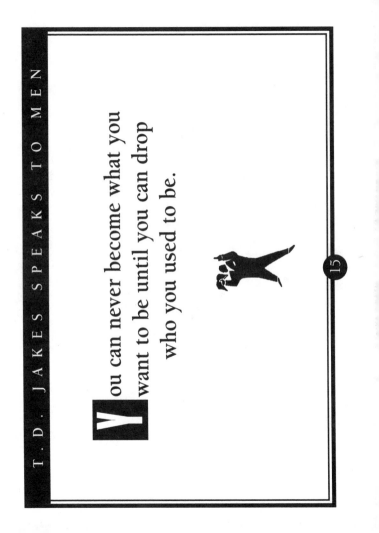

The greatest and most lethal weapon the enemy can ever challenge you with is YOU.

Thousands of men once believed they could never cheat on their income tax or their wives. But they did.

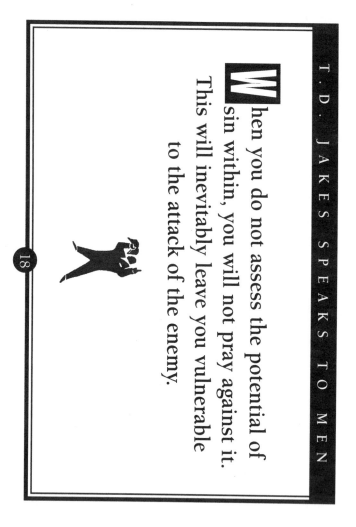

When you do not assess the potential of sin within, you will not pray against it. This will inevitably leave you vulnerable to the attack of the enemy.

Who are you when nobody is looking? That is the real you. Who are you really?

God has given you a marvelous gift.
He has given you life. What are
you going to do with it?

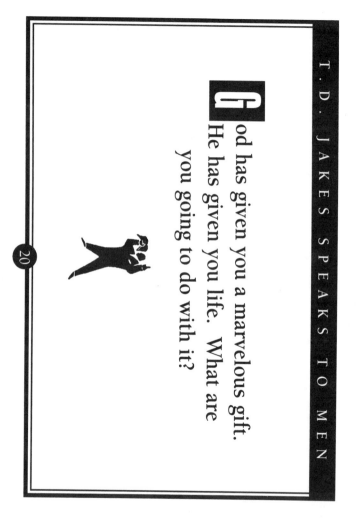

God's way is to tell it like it is. He doesn't put a bandage on your infected wound — He demands that the problem be dealt with.

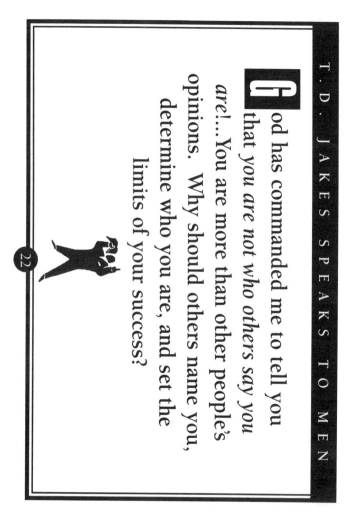

God has commanded me to tell you that *you are not who others say you are!*...You are more than other people's opinions. Why should others name you, determine who you are, and set the limits of your success?

This is not the day for the sniveling, weeping, weak, limp-wristed, emasculated man. This is the day for the leaping, jumping, rejoicing, resourceful man! Leap out! God has a plan for you.

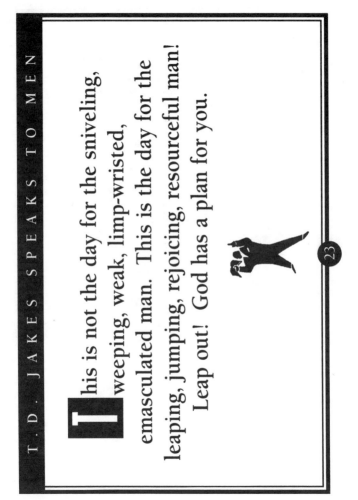

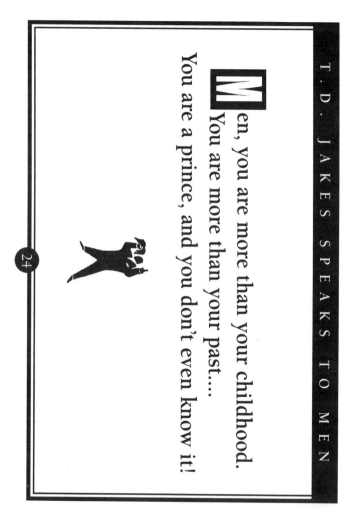

Men, you are more than your childhood.
You are more than your past....
You are a prince, and you don't even know it!

If you face your past because you want your future, God will open up the windows of heaven and pour you out a blessing!

Christian man, you are a prince, and the devil knows it. That's why he's been

trying to assassinate you.

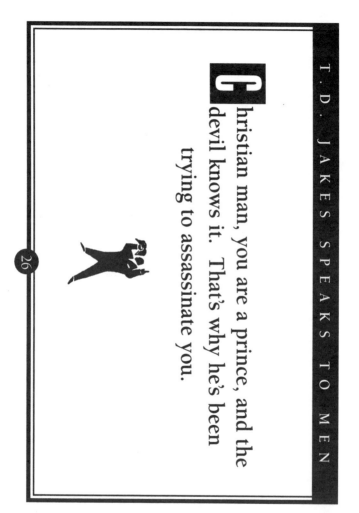

The enemy knows what you can be, and he wants to destroy you before you become what God said you will be.

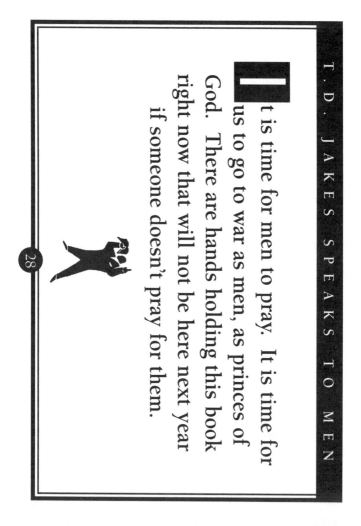

I t is time for men to pray. It is time for us to go to war as men, as princes of God. There are hands holding this book right now that will not be here next year if someone doesn't pray for them.

The turbulence of change can be over-powering. Satan does not want men to change. So if you are going to have peace in the process, you must guard your heart and mind with prayer.

Change isn't cheap. It will cost you a "death to the old" in order to experience a "birth to the new."

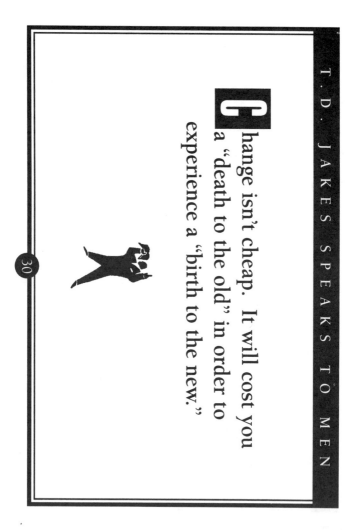

We need to celebrate our manhood from our first entrance into adulthood — to the end of our "grandfather phase." We need to receive instruction about our God-given responsibilities. We need to celebrate who we are in God's plan.

There may be a lot of people who don't want to give you a chance to change. But God is not like people. Every morning that you open your eyes and fill your lungs with air, God gives you another chance to change.

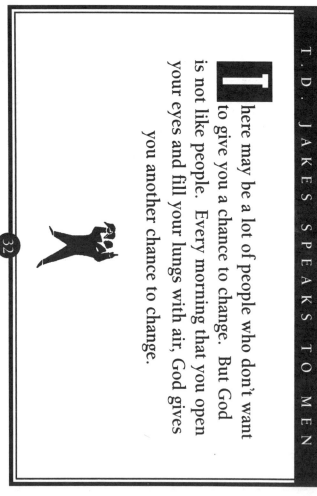

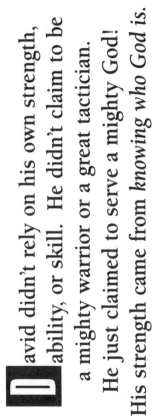

David didn't rely on his own strength, ability, or skill. He didn't claim to be a mighty warrior or a great tactician. He just claimed to serve a mighty God! His strength came from *knowing who God is*.

D avid tapped into the true source of manhood. His strength didn't come from male hormones or his male-dominant culture. It flowed from God's supernatural source.

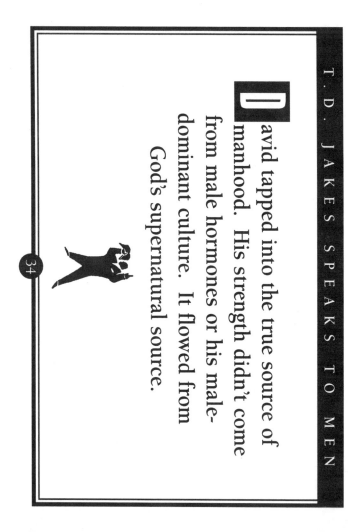

David showed us the right way to love true friends. He openly loved Jonathan, without any taint of homosexuality. We're so uptight that we can't even touch one another — except for a slap on the rear after a great play on the football field.

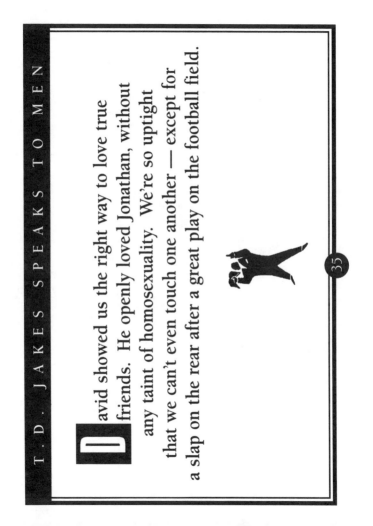

We need to model masculinity before our sons and help them celebrate their developing manhood.

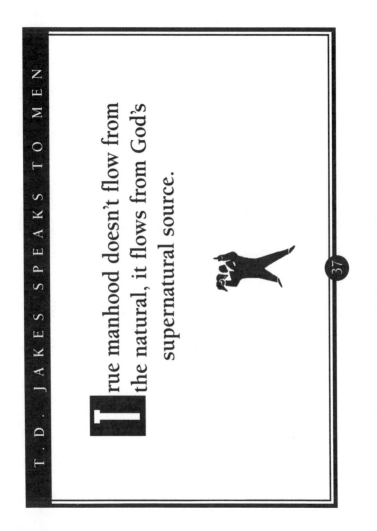

True manhood doesn't flow from the natural, it flows from God's supernatural source.

A true man inspires manhood in others.

One absolute prerequisite to the celebration of manhood is that there must be a *lion and a lamb* in every man.

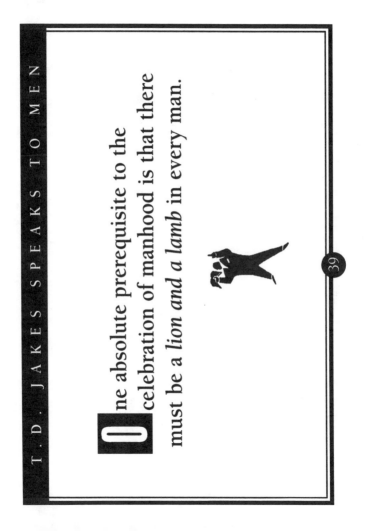

Jesus Christ was both God and man, lion and lamb. The art is to have both and know when to be which.

Generations are waiting to taste the fruit of your manly obedience and determination today.

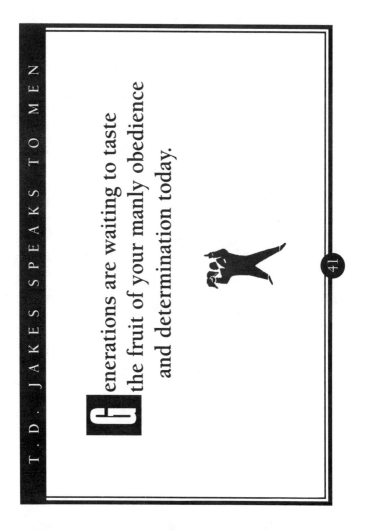

Our challenge as men is to overcome our reputation for being unable or unwilling to recognize problems in our relationships.

The greatest triumph in any man's life can be reduced to a mere monument of bitter rejection received through a withering remark or icy glance from a jealous wife.

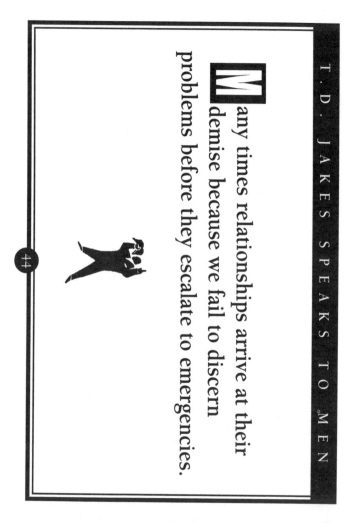

Many times relationships arrive at their demise because we fail to discern problems before they escalate to emergencies.

It is normal to expect your priorities and needs to change with time and maturity. But if you fail to keep your wife abreast of the changes within you, don't be surprised or upset if she continues to give you what you used to need and wonders why it isn't working anymore.

45

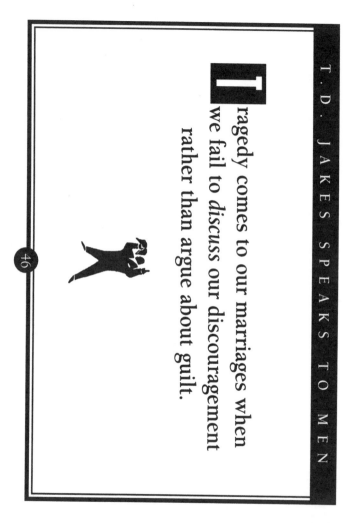

Tragedy comes to our marriages when we fail to *discuss* our discouragement rather than argue about guilt.

There is a difference between discussion and argument. A discussion airs the issues, but an argument alleges charges and appoints blame.

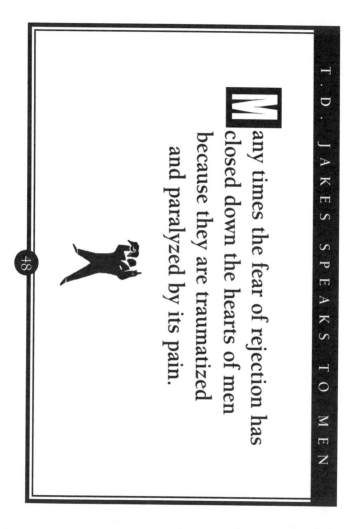

Many times the fear of rejection has closed down the hearts of men because they are traumatized and paralyzed by its pain.

We surround ourselves with images of success to hide our secret fears.

The greatest problems that can arise in our marriage is when we decide to become "marital missionaries." A marital missionary is a man who thinks he is called to change his wife — rather than to understand her!

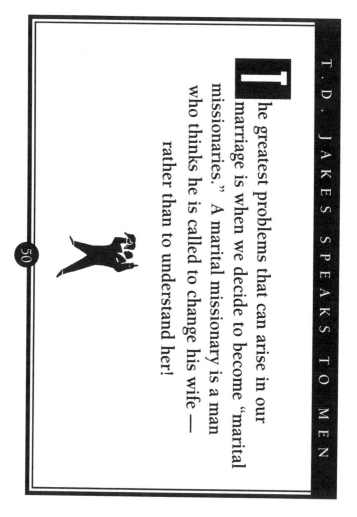

Men are masters at giving things. Where we have big problems is when we are asked to give *ourselves!* The real truth is that your wife doesn't need more things — she needs *you!*

I f you believe in the sovereignty of God, as I do, you know that God can make a bad decision turn out good. He can make a miracle out of a mistake.

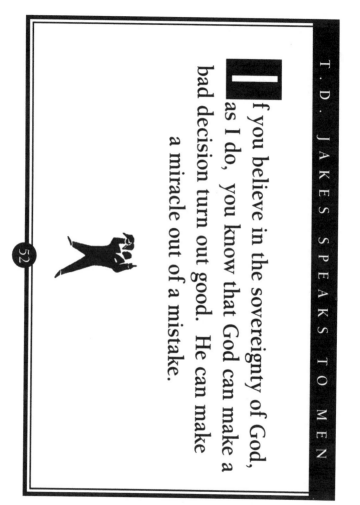

Y ou don't have to be a perfect performer. You don't even have to be a "ten." You just have to be a man. Your wife doesn't need to be a perfect "ten" either — or a "convert" to your image. She just has to be a woman, a genuine woman of God.

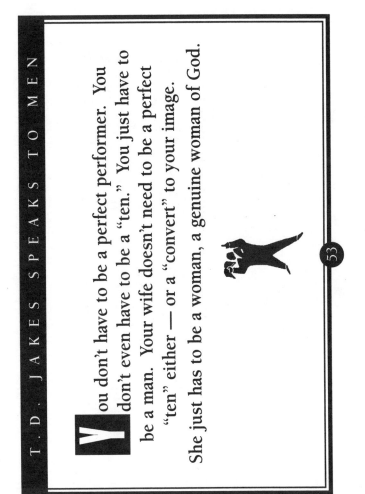

53

Cleaning up the messy problems of real-life men will force us to get personally involved with foul-smelling issues we don't even like to discuss. It is a laborious process, but *we need men who will loose men.*

If we want to touch men, then we must learn how to "adopt" one another. Some men desperately need to be fully accepted because they need to experience a relationship they never had in their childhood.

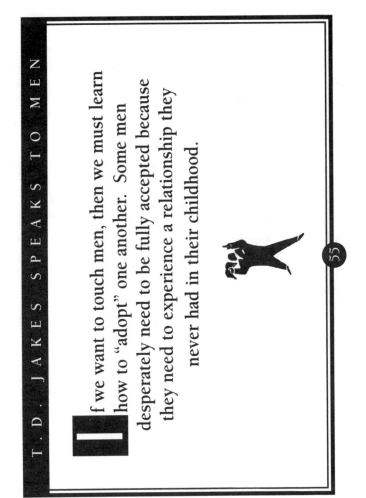

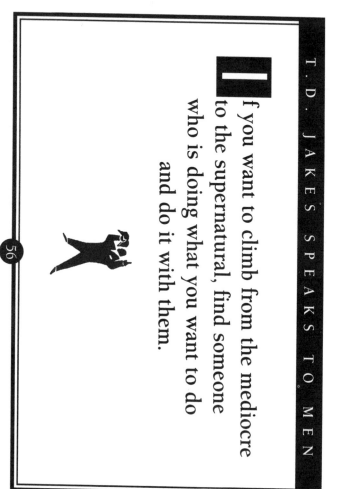

If you want to climb from the mediocre to the supernatural, find someone who is doing what you want to do and do it with them.

People can never give you what they have not received.

he greatest investment you can make is an investment in people! That's what God did. He invested His Son in humanity, and reaped the harvest of the Church.

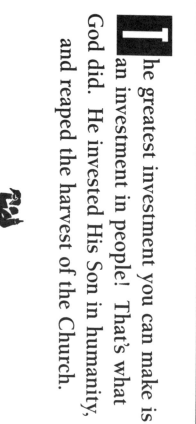

If you have achieved any level of success, pour it into someone else! Success is not success without a successor!

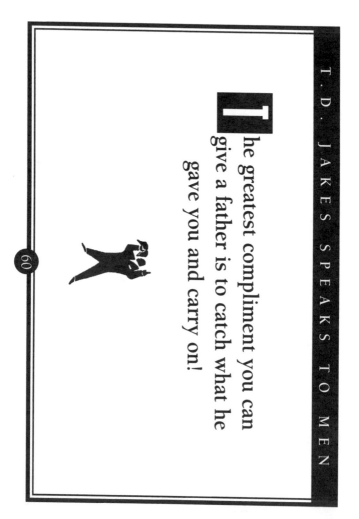

The greatest compliment you can give a father is to catch what he gave you and carry on!

60

If you feel you have outgrown your need for a father, then at least be a father. Somewhere there is a desperate young man whose natural ties are broken. Bind him and train him. Teach him and pour into him all the things you want to say to the next generation!

Our Savior keeps His commitment to men who have been discarded and buried by others. He is a God of relationship, and His creation can never escape its need for intimacy with its Creator.

The same confident men who are so tough and brash and brawny elsewhere — these master negotiators of the workplace find themselves nervous and anxious about facing the 110-pound woman who waits for them at home!

Men have merely *reacted* long enough. Now it's time to *act*.

God wants strong men who lead instead of weak men who only follow.

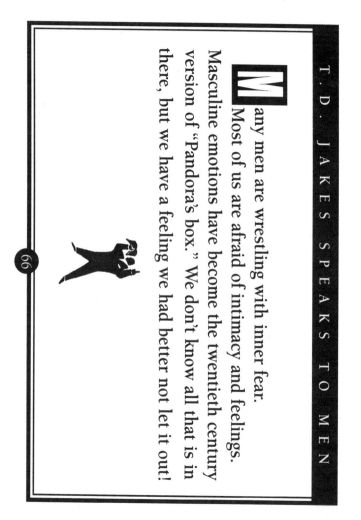

Many men are wrestling with inner fear. Most of us are afraid of intimacy and feelings. Masculine emotions have become the twentieth century version of "Pandora's box." We don't know all that is in there, but we have a feeling we had better not let it out!

Man of God, *you have been robbed!* The enemy has stolen the warm, giddy feeling of excitement out of your heart! Do you want it back? Fight for it! Recall the soft songs, light those fragrant candles, take those long walks of longing, and once again murmur passionate words in your mate's ear.

Take back what the enemy is trying to steal from you.

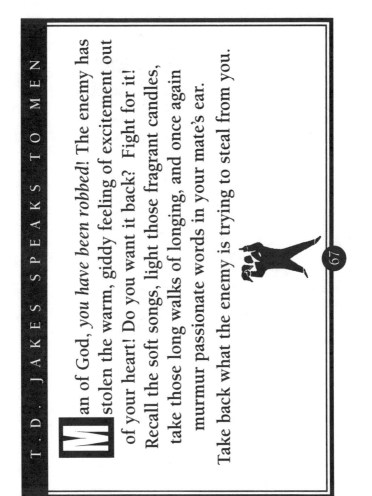

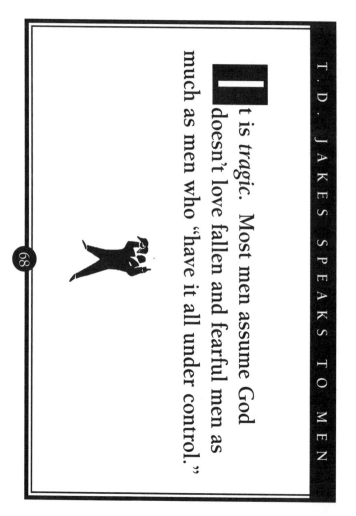

It is *tragic*. Most men assume God doesn't love fallen and fearful men as much as men who "have it all under control."

You can't have genuine friendships
if you hide your true self.

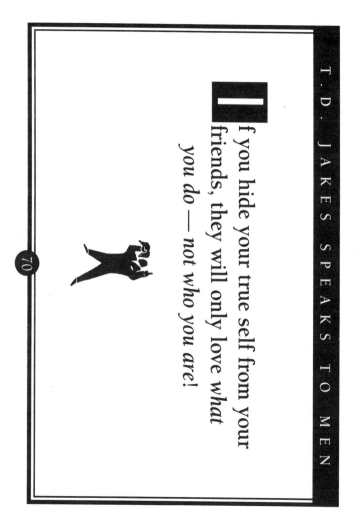

If you hide your true self from your friends, they will only love what you do — *not who you are!*

Most of your jobs and relationships have been built on your personal performance and achievement, but God's call is not like that. All He wants is you.

Jesus was the Only One who was willing to die to be your Friend!

Once you understand that God is committed to you, loneliness is impossible.

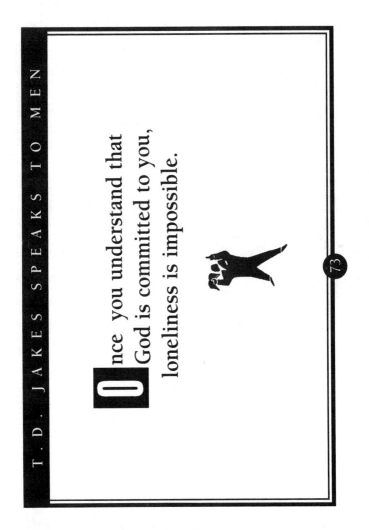

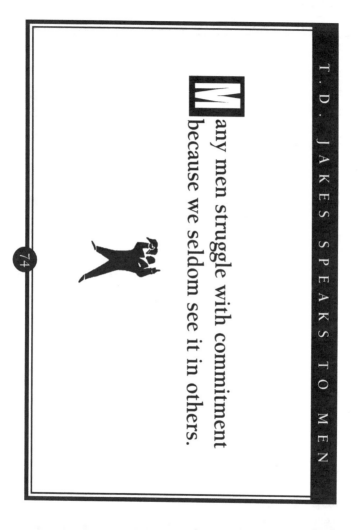

Many men struggle with commitment because we seldom see it in others.

The hand of God is warm and tender, yet firm and strong. It is there for every dark night, for every tainted secret, and for every wounded marriage! God wipes away the hidden tears we never allowed to fall.

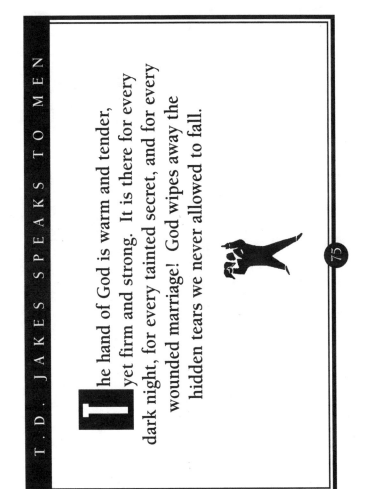

75

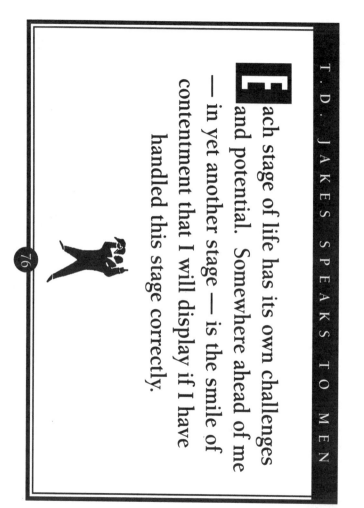

Each stage of life has its own challenges and potential. Somewhere ahead of me — in yet another stage — is the smile of contentment that I will display if I have handled this stage correctly.

If you want some good advice, don't take the opinions of others too seriously.

Whoever comes after you should have it easier than you did because blessed people always leave a blessing!

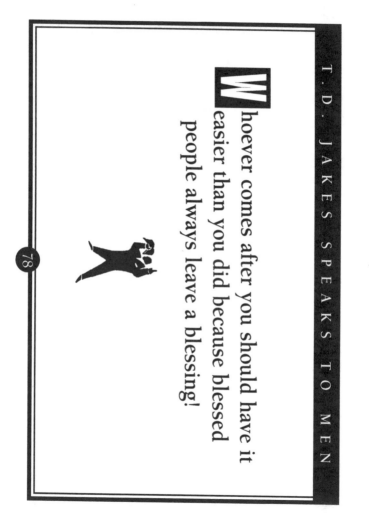

Teach your children wisdom. Teach them how to make and handle money without worshipping it!

Excellent leadership always works itself out of a job!

Stagnancy is the enemy of progression.

How can we condemn abortion and shun women with illegitimate children?

How can we condemn divorce and fail to teach and practice restoration for damaged marriages?

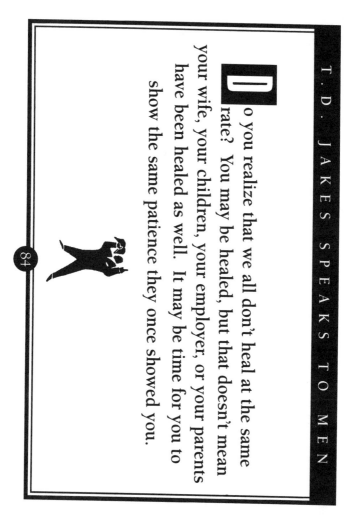

D o you realize that we all don't heal at the same rate? You may be healed, but that doesn't mean your wife, your children, your employer, or your parents have been healed as well. It may be time for you to show the same patience they once showed you.

Remember to comfort rather than criticize.

The wisest of men are those who recognize their need to change.

Have the courage to face the uncertainty of *new* beginnings with a deep commitment to succeed!

Most Christian men pray like wimps and brag like warriors. The truth is that real spiritual warriors are men who pray.

Don't avoid prayer because you think you are not articulate or expressive. The stumbling, bumbling words of a tear-stained heart ring out louder in the spirit realm than the finest resonating voice of an orator.

Prayer is a compliment to God. It is an admission that we believe in His competence to deal with the issues.

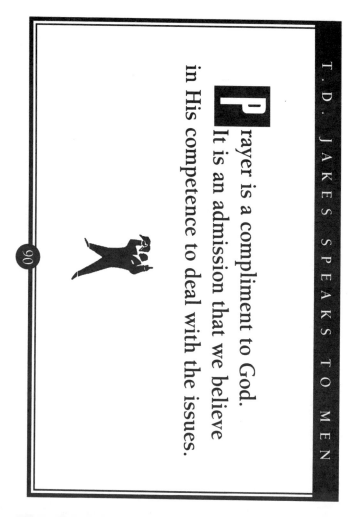

Your greatest message to your son is the one he sees, not the one he hears.

Man of God, *I dare you to kneel down and pray!* Don't ask God to fix "them"; ask Him to fix you, and He will heal the land.

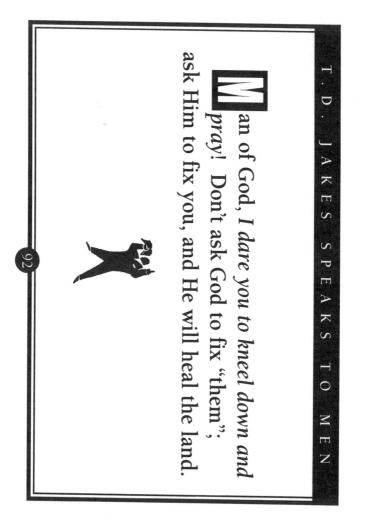

Obedience is the highest form of praise.

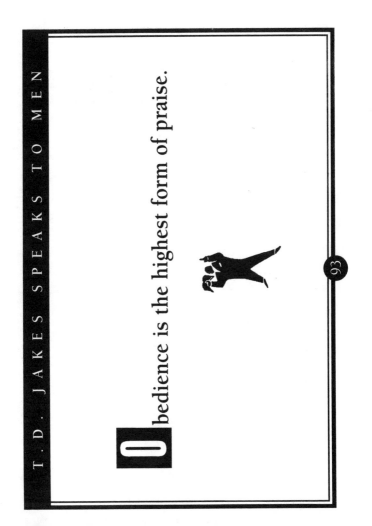

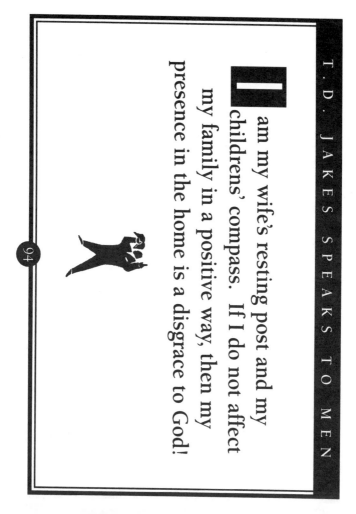

I am my wife's resting post and my childrens' compass. If I do not affect my family in a positive way, then my presence in the home is a disgrace to God!

I want to set a standard of excellence that is so high I won't be afraid for my daughters to marry "someone like their father."

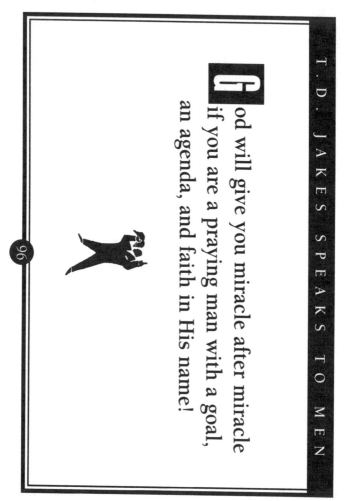

God will give you miracle after miracle if you are a praying man with a goal, an agenda, and faith in His name!

**T**here *are some things you give to no one but God.* Always reserve the deepest and innermost portion of your heart and trust for God.

Tell the enemy, "I am a man of prayer. I will be knocked no lower than my knees!"

Giving is an opportunity to share the fruits of your undeserved blessing with a deserving God who has been gracious to you.

Resurrection changes the way you react to fear and death. It doesn't mean you will never fear again. It simply means you will forever react to fear differently.

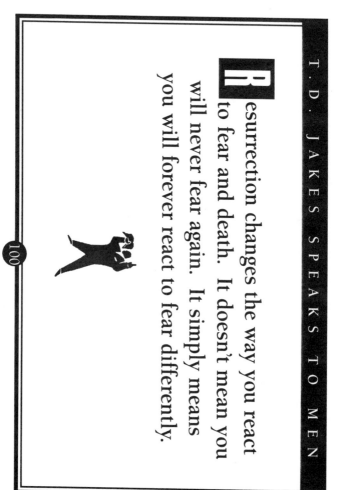

Survival breeds confidence.

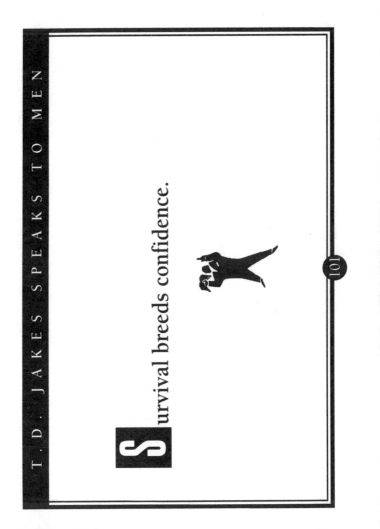

God never says "if" when He talks about your destiny.

The devil is deathly afraid of a *loosed man*!

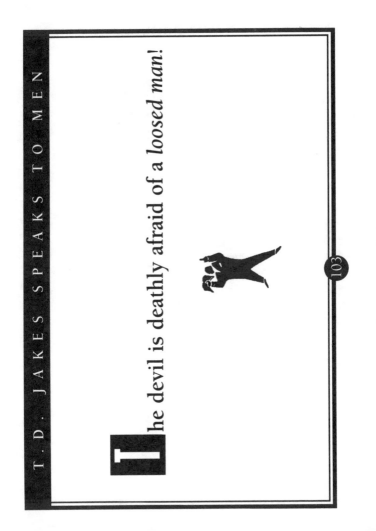

Jesus told Simon, "When thou art converted, strengthen thy brethren." A loosed man always reaches back for others.

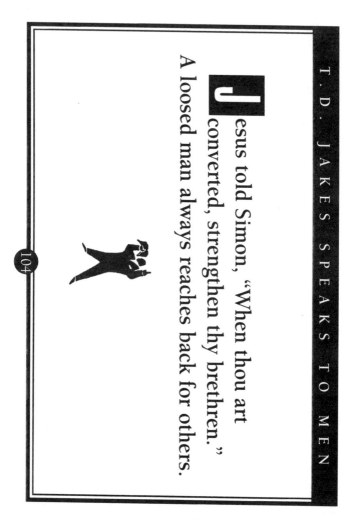

Although God had made a wonderful place for Adam to live, the man remained less than complete. He needed a woman. Keep in mind, though, that she completed his *purpose*, not his *person*. If you're not complete as a person, marriage will not help you.

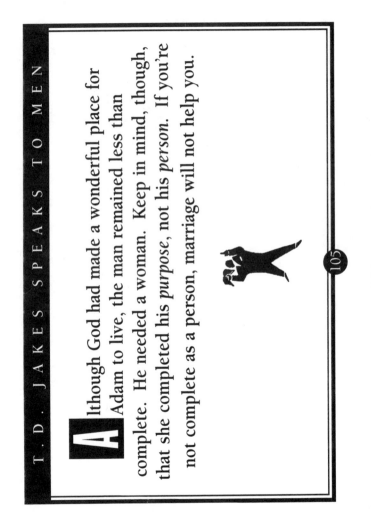

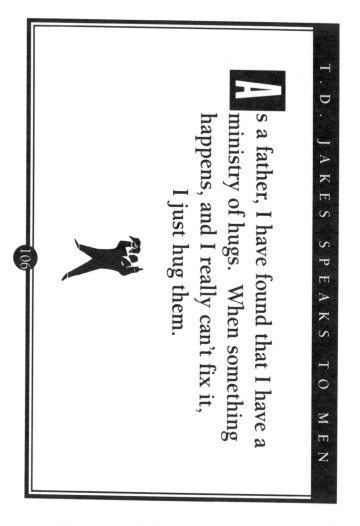

As a father, I have found that I have a ministry of hugs. When something happens, and I really can't fix it, I just hug them.

Christ is not an impotent, weak, unresponsive, incompetent force. He is a God of power. He is revolutionary. He is life-changing. He is able to affect circumstances and situations.

We need to send a signal that reverberates across the world. Our Lord is not dead! He has all power in His hands! And when His people get together — not only can we rent auditoriums — we can buy them!

You cannot legislate love. Don't look to the White House. Don't look to the ballot box. Don't even look to the Church House. Look to getting on your knees before God.

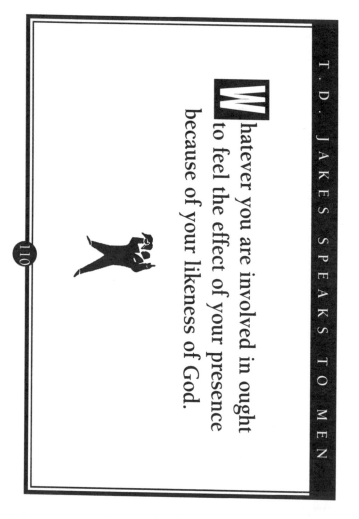

Whatever you are involved in ought to feel the effect of your presence because of your likeness of God.

When you decide to help somebody, you won't have to carry them forever. Just get them to Jesus.

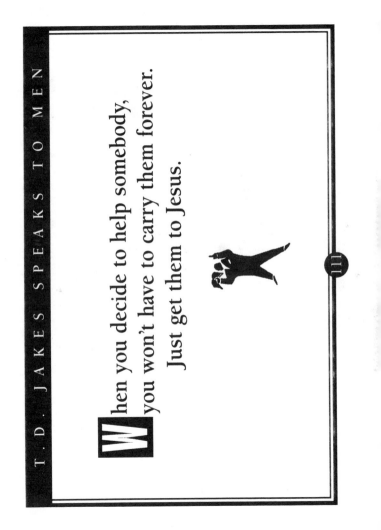

David said, "When my heart is overwhelmed, *lead me to the rock!*"

Men have an appointment with a miracle. The Spirit of the Lord wants to do a work in our lives.

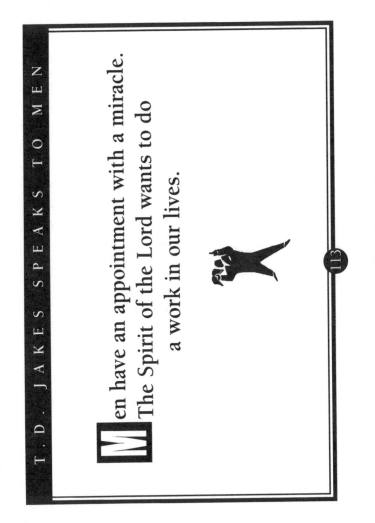

Have you been in church so long that you've forgotten what you came for?

What has happened to this generation? When I was a little boy, we were afraid to walk into crowds of men. Now men are afraid to walk into crowds of boys.

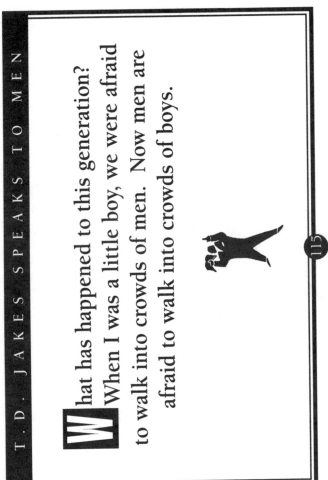

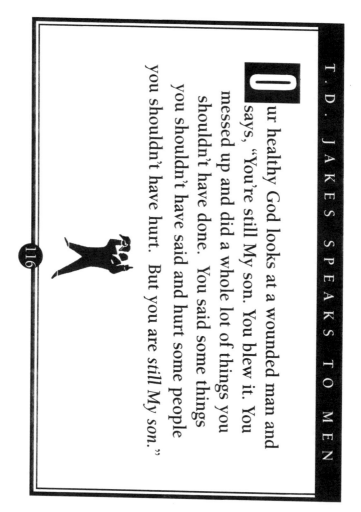

Our healthy God looks at a wounded man and says, "You're still My son. You blew it. You messed up and did a whole lot of things you shouldn't have done. You said some things you shouldn't have said and hurt some people you shouldn't have hurt. But you are still My son."

Real deliverance is when you take control
of the thing that had control of you.

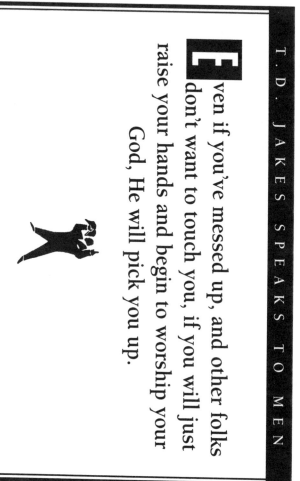

Even if you've messed up, and other folks don't want to touch you, if you will just raise your hands and begin to worship your God, He will pick you up.

The move of God cannot be contained. It can be criticized and frustrated, but it cannot be contained.

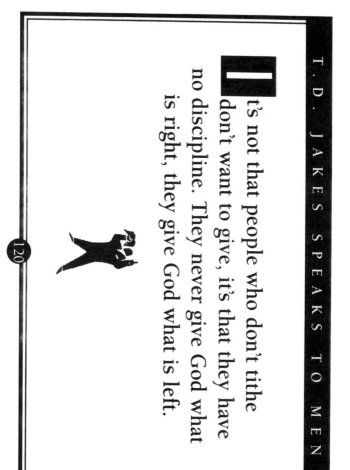

It's not that people who don't tithe don't want to give, it's that they have no discipline. They never give God what is right, they give God what is left.

Even if you don't have money and can't give, don't despise an offering. If you can't sing, you don't despise the choir. So don't despise an offering. Lack of money is only a temporary circumstance.

You better plan on getting old, because you either do it or die.

A blessed man is in authority and under authority.

No woman wants to be in submission to a man who isn't in submission to God.

A man who cannot rule his own spirit is like a city without walls. A man with no walls will let anything in.

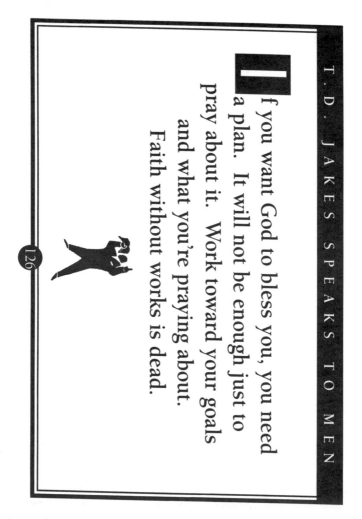

If you want God to bless you, you need a plan. It will not be enough just to pray about it. Work toward your goals and what you're praying about. Faith without works is dead.

When your life is on hold and you think you're waiting on God, I've got news for you. You're not waiting on God, He's waiting on you.

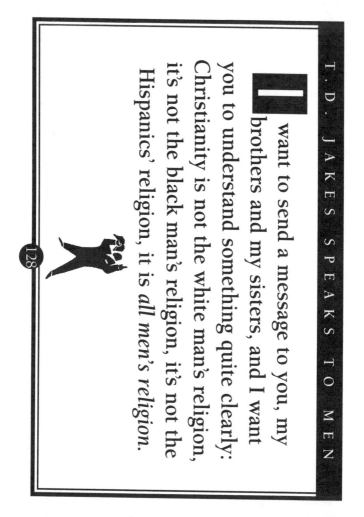

I want to send a message to you, my brothers and my sisters, and I want you to understand something quite clearly: Christianity is not the white man's religion, it's not the black man's religion, it's not the Hispanics' religion, it is *all men's religion*.

Christianity is not for wimps.
It's for *real* men.

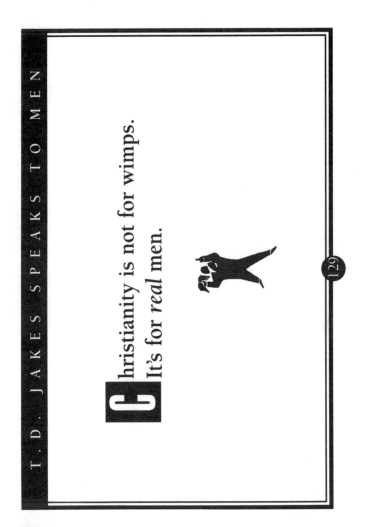

Man was the only thing in creation that God touched to create.

Faith for the believer is what gasoline is for an automobile.

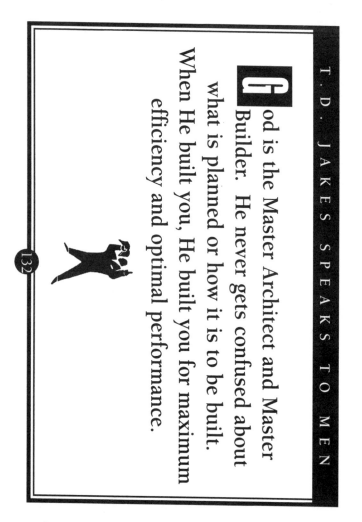

God is the Master Architect and Master Builder. He never gets confused about what is planned or how it is to be built. When He built you, He built you for maximum efficiency and optimal performance.

Good has a way of taking people who have been forsaken by men and raising them up. In fact, God *prefers* such individuals, because when they get into a place of power, they are not arrogant like those who think they deserve to be there.

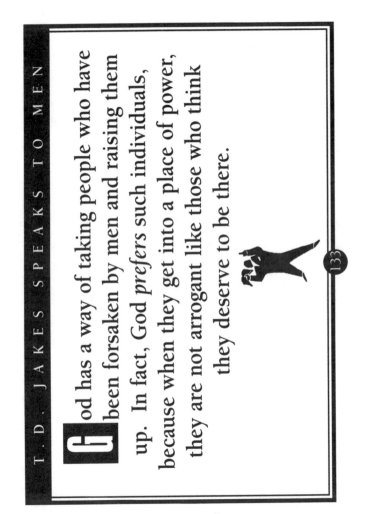

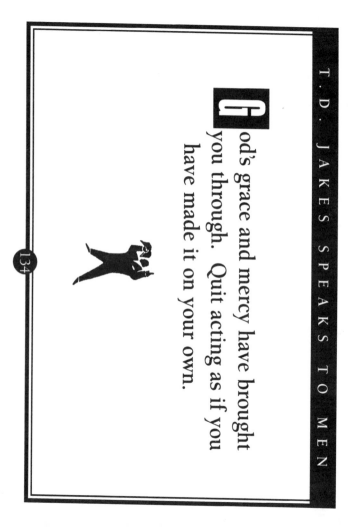

God's grace and mercy have brought you through. Quit acting as if you have made it on your own.

A tremendous amount of power is released when we praise.

W hen you take God's thoughts and enter into praise, you become like a battering ram against the strongholds that Satan has erected in your mind.

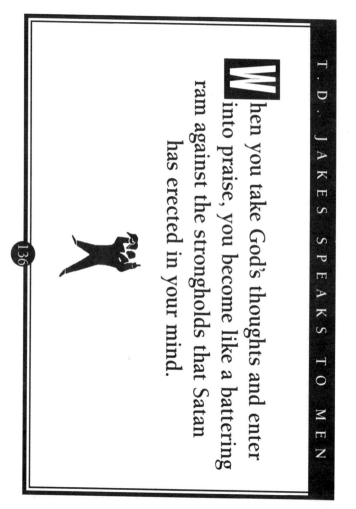

Whatever we worship is what we ultimately end up serving.

It's not enough for us to go to church together. We're not really brothers until we can laugh and cry together.

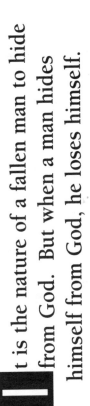

I t is the nature of a fallen man to hide from God. But when a man hides himself from God, he loses himself.

Trusting God with your successes isn't really a challenge. The real test of trust is to be able to share your secrets, your inner failures and fears.

Mutual enhancement comes into a relationship where there is intimacy based on honesty.

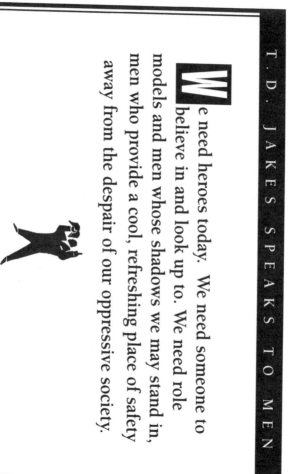

We need heroes today. We need someone to believe in and look up to. We need role models and men whose shadows we may stand in, men who provide a cool, refreshing place of safety away from the despair of our oppressive society.

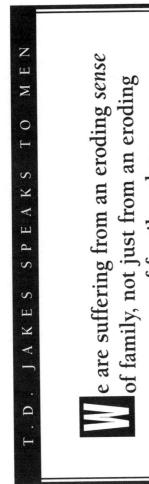

We are suffering from an eroding *sense* of family, not just from an eroding sense of family values.

143

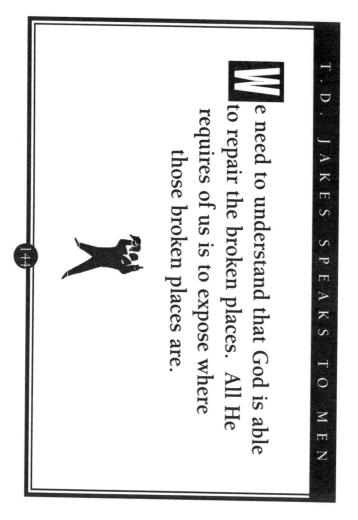

We need to understand that God is able to repair the broken places. All He requires of us is to expose where those broken places are.

It takes great courage to exemplify total honesty with God.

When we discover our own limitations, we become eligible to discover the all-sufficiency of God.

The call of God is a high calling. Yet it has been answered by lowly men who have had the discernment to see a God high and lifted up.

There can be no fulfillment where there is no passion.

Jesus Christ, the greatest lover the world has ever known, gives Himself openly and unashamedly.

His love is exemplified in His coming, but is consummated in His dying.

Undirected passion becomes a spawning bed for perversity and dankness. It is *what we do with what we feel* that controls the direction of our lives.

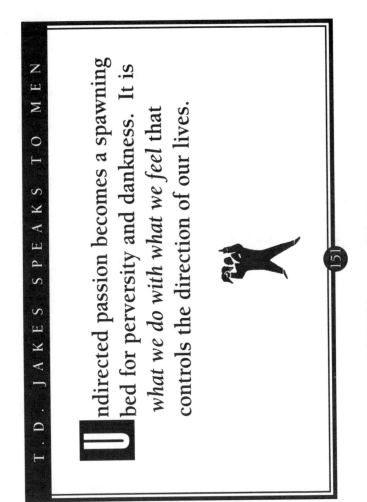

There is nothing more hollow than empty words and lofty clichés that have no real meaning or compassion in them.

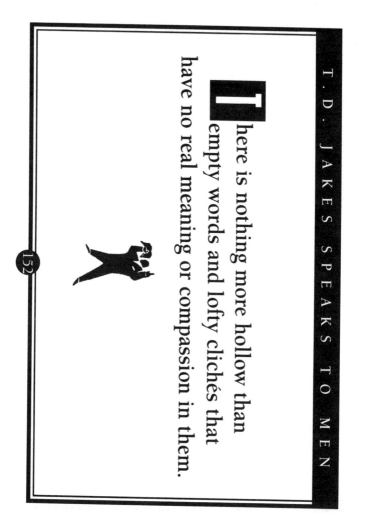

Do you know that many times your *thoughts* need to be healed? We must understand that modern medicine can heal many afflictions of the body, but only God Himself can heal the mind.

One of the great challenges of our walk with God is to resist the temptation to allow what happened in the past determine who we are today.

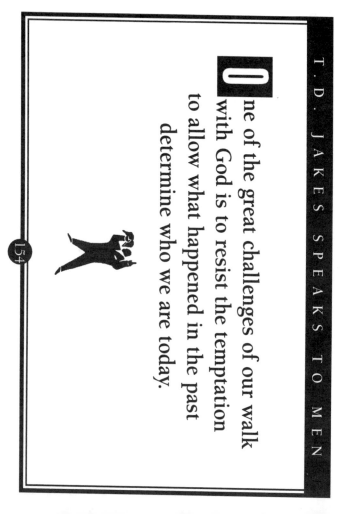

Thoughts are previews of coming attractions.

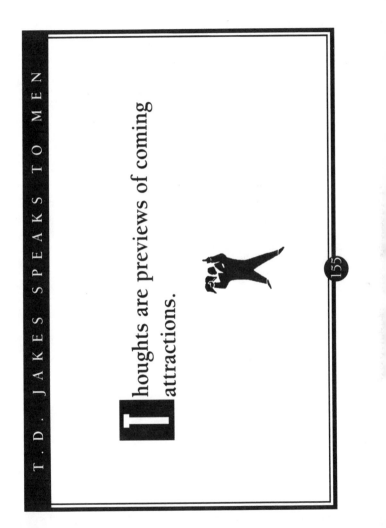

As we hear the thoughts of God, His thinking becomes increasingly contagious.

In a world where people seem void of commitment and become so easily distracted, it is comforting to know that God won't give up on you.

About the Author

T.D. Jakes is the senior pastor and founder of Temple of Faith Ministries in Charleston, West Virginia. Transcending all social and gender barriers, his message of healing and restoration is broadcast nationally into millions of homes. Bishop Jakes ministers frequently in massive crusades and conferences across this nation. He is also a highly celebrated author.

To contact T.D. Jakes write:

Jakes Ministries
P.O. Box 7056
Charleston, West Virginia 25356

Additional copies of this book and other book titles
from **ALBURY PUBLISHING** are
available at your local bookstore.

Albury Publishing
P.O. Box 470406
Tulsa, Oklahoma 74147-0406